2020

Key West
& the Florida Keys

Restaurants

The Food Enthusiast's
Long Weekend Guide

Andrew Delaplaine

*Andrew Delaplaine is the Food Enthusiast.
When he's not playing tennis,
he dines anonymously
at the Publisher's expense.*

WANT 3 *FREE* THRILLERS?

Why, of course you do!
If you like these writers--
Vince Flynn, Brad Thor, Tom Clancy, James Patterson,
David Baldacci, John Grisham, Brad Meltzer, Daniel
Silva, Don DeLillo
If you like these TV series –
House of Cards, Scandal, West Wing, The Good Wife,
Madam Secretary, Designated Survivor

You'll love the **unputdownable** series about
Jack Houston St. Clair, with political intrigue, romance,
and loads of action and suspense.

Besides writing travel books, I've written political thrillers
for many years that have delighted hundreds of thousands
of readers. I want to introduce you to my work!
Send me an email and I'll send you a link where you can
download the first 3 books in my bestselling series,
absolutely FREE.

Mention **this book** when you email me.
andrewdelaplaine@mac.com

Key West & the Florida Keys

TABLE OF CONTENTS

Gramercy Park Press
New York – London - Paris

Chapter 1
KEY WEST &
THE FLORIDA KEYS

Most people's idea of a vacation involves sun, sand and sea. The Florida Keys have it all and more. If you are traveling to Key West, you must drive down at least once. After that one drive, you can fly down, but you have to experience this drive at least once in your life. It's not one of the most famous drives in the world for nothing.

The incomparable views of both the Atlantic Ocean and the Gulf of Mexico will accompany you throughout your drive. Sometimes, admiring these clear warm waters is not enough. Soon after you pass Key Largo in the Upper Keys, the urge to stop and jump into the water will strike you. No worries, there are plenty of areas along the way where you can pull over and do just that. At times, the water is so shallow you will be walking far out and the warm waters will barely reach knee level. Back in the days when I was an avid scuba diver, we'd stop two or three times along the drive to Key West, fill our tanks at one of the roadside scuba shops, and go diving that very minute.

Also along the way you will find attractions and activities for just about everyone. From shipwreck museums, to shopping, to haunted houses, to water sports.

Restaurants offer an abundance of seafood cooked up in a variety of ways. I try to make it a rule to avoid all meats when I go to the Keys. The seafood is so good, so fresh, and so well prepared (even in the simplest crab shack) that you really shouldn't be eating burgers and steaks.

Nightlife in the Keys pretty much means bars, bars and more bars. People here DO like to drink. And you'll still see "rummies" here and there. These are people who have given up on life and migrated to the

Keys where the pace of life slows to a crawl, to a rum-induced haze.

Speaking of that pace, it's something you'll notice right away. Things do move at a much slower pace than most people are used to. Here, you will be forced to relax. Whether you want to or not. I remember once I was in a hurry to get to a party at the Pier house in Key West. I was flying down from my office in Miami. It was a hot, muggy summer night. I dashed out of the airport and hopped into a cab and told the driver to "Hurry! I need to get to the Pier House right away!" The bearded, aging, burned-out hippy driver looked at me in the rearview mirror and said, "Okay, then, I'll go the long way. There's no rush in Key West," he pontificated. And he poked along at 20 mph. I wanted to kill him, but I got the message. This was many years ago, before there were any hotel chain properties in Key West. Before things went "corporate." Back when it was real.

Chapter 2
TIPS FOR GETTING AROUND

The Mile Marker Address System
Along US 1 (also called the Overseas Highway),
you'll see these small green signs along the way that
start when you leave Florida City at the top of the

Keys, with Mile Marker 126. The last Mile Marker is MM 0, which is in Key West. Many businesses give their address as "MM 56," for instance, which mean Mile Marker 56.

Basic Tip
My rule for transport about the Keys is simple: if you're in Key West, you don't need a car. If you're exploring the Upper and Middle Keys, why then of course you can't do without one. So if you're flying into Key West, do not rent a car once you get there. You simply will not need one. Cabs are plentiful. And nothing is more than a 5-minute cab ride away.

Similarly, if I drive down to Key West, the minute I get there I park the car and leave it, using cabs throughout my stay. When it's busy, parking is a nightmare (just like it is on South Beach, where I live), so I'm never hassled trying to park if I use cabs.

However, if you are staying on some of the larger keys or in Key West, there will be a variety of scooter rental places available. These scooter rental places also offer a variety of golf cart rentals that can accommodate different size parties from 2 people up to 6.

Beware Speed Traps
A lot of municipalities along the Overseas Highway set up speed traps which are designed primarily to raise revenue from unsuspecting tourists. So you've been warned. They usually don't give a damn if you're 3 miles or 15 over the limit. They just want

your money. One place where you really ought to slow down, however, is Big Pine Key where the **National Key Deer Refuge** is located. This is the habitat of a small population of "Key deer," a small (and very cute) animal that's in serious danger (150 were killed by cars last year).

SPECIFIC INFORMATION DURING YOUR VISIT

The best you can do here is just ask one of the friendly locals for events and local points of interest. Some of the larger keys have local publications that will offer information about events taking place during the time you are there.

http://hometownkeywest.com/events/

VISITOR'S CENTERS

The following chambers of commerce will provide specific information about local businesses and services along with discount coupons and promotions in the general area. You can also get maps and information on the local cultural scene, such as it is.

FLORIDA KEYS VISITOR CENTER
106240 Overseas Hwy, Key Largo, 305-712-6596
www.keylargochamber.org/about-us/

GREATER MARATHON CHAMBER OF COMMERCE
12222 Overseas Hwy, Marathon: 305-743-5417
www.floridakeysmarathon.com/

ISLAMORADA CHAMBER OF COMMERCE
87100 Overseas Hwy, Mile Marker 87, Bayside, 305-664-4503
www.islamoradachamber.com/

KEY LARGO CHAMBER OF COMMERCE
106000 Overseas Hwy, Key Largo: 305-451-1414
www.keylargochamber.org/about-us/

MONROE COUNTY TOURISM SITE
www.fla-keys.com/keylargo/

KEY WEST CHAMBER OF COMMERCE
510 Greene St., 1st Floor, Key West: 305-294-2587
www.keywestchamber.org/

LOWER KEYS CHAMBER OF COMMERCE
U.S. 1 at MM 31, Big Pine Key: 305-872-2411
www.lowerkeyschamber.com/

Chapter 3
UPPER & MIDDLE KEYS

DID YOU FIND AN INTERESTING PLACE?
If you discover a place you think I should check out on my next visit, drop me a line, will you? I'll mention your name if I end up listing it.
andrewdelaplaine@mac.com

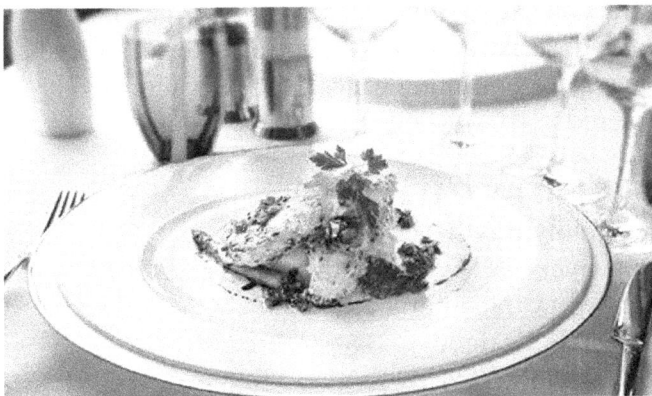

ALABAMA JACKS
58000 Card Sound Rd., Key Largo: 305-248-8741
No web site

CUISINE: Seafood
DRINKS: Full bar
SERVING: Daily lunch and dinner
PRICE RANGE: $
One of the best places in all the Keys for conch fritters, certainly in the Upper Keys. Don't let the bikers at the other tables scare you. They're pretty much harmless unless you speak out of turn.

BARRACUDA GRILL
4290 Overseas Hwy. at MM 49.5, Marathon: 305-743-3314
www.barracuda-grill.com/
CUISINE: American/ Seafood
DRINKS: Beer/ Wine
SERVING: Dinner
PRICE RANGE: $$$-$$$
Small and casual, this spot serves really good seafood, steaks and chops. They offer a well-priced wine list of California wines. No reservations required.

BUTTERFLY CAFÉ
Tranquility Bay Beach House Resort
2600 Overseas Hwy., Marathon: 305-289-7177
http://www.tranquilitybay.com
CUISINE: Seafood
DRINKS: Beer/ Wine
SERVING: Breakfast/ Lunch/ Dinner
PRICE RANGE: $$-$$$
Inside the Tranquility Bay Resort, this place offers incredible water views and an even better menu. The Sunday brunch is particularly good.

CALYPSO'S SEAFOOD GRILL

1 Seagate Blvd. at MM 99.5, Key Largo: 305-451-0600

http://calypsoskeylargo.com/index.html

CUISINE: Seafood

DRINKS: Beer/ Wine

SERVING: Lunch/Dinner

PRICE RANGE: $

Typical Keys eatery on the water with loud music and good food. The she-crab soup is a must. Other specialties are cracked conch and steamed clams. Great food at really great prices.

CHEF MICHAEL'S

81671 Overseas Hwy, Islamorada, 305-664-0640

http://www.foodtotalkabout.com

CUISINE: Seafood / Vegetarian / Vegan
DRINKS: Beer & wine
SERVING: Dinner nightly, Sunday Brunch
PRICE RANGE: $$$
There are a lot of pathetically crappy restaurants in
the Middle and Lower Keys (does the beer have to be
that bad in so many places? Or the conch fritters
heavy with batter and low on conch?), but this isn't
one of them. This upscale eatery offers Chef
Michael's creative menu of seafood & New American
entrees close enough to the **Cheeca Lodge** that you
can walk over. The dining room is small and intimate,
seating under 30, but there's room for that many more
outside on the porch. Menu picks include Hogfish (a
specialty) and their infamous French toast for Sunday
brunch. Great fish selections chosen from whatever
local fishermen bring the chef that day, so you might
get yellowtail, swordfish, grouper, tripletail, tuna—
whatever they bring—and get it served either sautéed,
grilled, blackened or fried. Dessert standouts are the
really fine Key Lime Pie and the crème brulee made
daily.

GILBERT'S RESORT TIKI BAR
107900 Overseas Hwy., Key Largo: 305-451-1133
gilbertsresort.com
CUISINE: German, Seafood
DRINKS: Full bar
SERVING: Daily lunch and dinner
PRICE RANGE: $$
This is perhaps the very first place in the Keys where
you can experience that special laid-back feeling that
people associate with the Keys. Barely anybody

knows about it. Just a bit south of Homestead, just when you go into the Keys on Key Largo, you take the first right and you'll find yourself here at Gilbert's. If you see a sunset here, and you've never been to the Keys before, you'll want to continue south. Only 45 minutes from Miami (without traffic). Chef Georg Schu is from Germany, and this is the only place I know down here that serves German specialties (as well as local seafood).

GREEN TURTLE INN
81219 Overseas Hwy. at MM 81.2, Islamorada: 305-664-2006
www.greenturtleinn.com/
CUISINE: Seafood
DRINKS: Full Bar
SERVING: Breakfast/ Lunch/ Dinner
PRICE RANGE: $$$
Great little eatery that offers a gourmet market and dishes cooked with locally farmed produce and microgreens. For lunch they have an excellent fried green tomato BLT and at breakfast, their coconut French toast is a must. Check out the art gallery and gourmet shop.

HARRIETTE'S RESTAURANT
95710 Overseas Hwy. at MM 95.7, Key Largo: 305-852-8689
https://www.facebook.com/HarriettesRestaurant
CUISINE: Breakfast/ Brunch
DRINKS: No alcohol
SERVING: Breakfast
PRICE RANGE: $

Open only for breakfast (until 2 pm) this place packs in a major crowd. On a diet? No problem. Aside from their enormous homemade biscuits and muffins, this place offers a South Beach Diet and Atkins diet menu. (But I've never had any of the diet foods—the breakfasts are too good, especially the hash browns.)

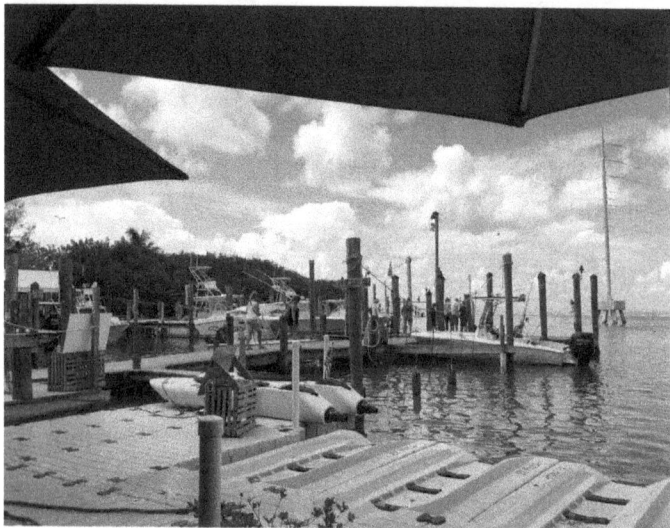

HUNGRY TARPON

77522 Overseas Hwy, Islamorada, 305-664-0535
www.hungrytarpon.com
CUISINE: Seafood / Caribbean
DRINKS: Full Bar
SERVING: Lunch & Dinner
PRICE RANGE: $$
Casual seafood shack with a bayside deck—just what everybody's image is of a little waterfront eatery in the Keys. They have a great blackened grouper sandwich. Great food offerings but you can also

bring your own catch to be cooked by the chef. Restaurant is surrounded by artisan kiosks and a bait and tackle shop.

ISLAMORADA FISH COMPANY
81532 Overseas Hwy. at MM 81.5, Islamorada: 305-664-9271
http://www.islamoradafishco.com
CUISINE: Seafood
DRINKS: Full Bar
SERVING: Breakfast/ Lunch/ Dinner
PRICE RANGE: $
Don't let its average looks fool you, this place is serving up some incredible dishes including outstanding breakfasts. Keep your eyes on the water; manatees are known to drift by.

ISLAND GRILL
85501 Overseas Hwy. at MM 85, Islamorada: 305-664-8400
http://keysislandgrill.com
CUISINE: Seafood
DRINKS: Full Bar
SERVING: Breakfast/ Lunch/ Dinner
PRICE RANGE: $
Located just under the Snake Creek Bridge, this place has a sprawling outdoor deck and bar with intimate waterfront dining. Serving up fresh fish, shrimp and calamari; you can also bring your own catch and they will cook it up for you.

KAIYO GRILL & SUSHI

81701 Old Hwy. at MM 82, Islamorada: 305-664-5556

http://www.kaiyokeys.com

CUISINE: Japanese/ Sushi

DRINKS: Wine/ Sake

SERVING: Lunch/ Dinner

PRICE RANGE: $$$$

This eclectic, colorful restaurant looks completely out of place in the Keys but with their superb, contemporary sushi, people from all over South Florida are finding their way here. Although diners are casually dressed, the service is a notch above.

KEY LARGO CONCH HOUSE RESTAURANT & COFFEE BAR

100211 Overseas Hwy. at MM 100, Key Largo: 305-453-4844

www.keylargoconchhouse.com

CUISINE: American

DRINKS: Full Bar

SERVING: Breakfast/ Lunch/ Dinner

PRICE RANGE: $

Featured on the Food Network, the Conch House is exactly that, a house set amidst lush landscaping with great food priced right. A local hotspot, this is a pet friendly eatery. This family-owned spot is a favorite among locals for the quality of its conch fritters, and they even host an annual Conch Fritter Eating Contest awarding laurels to whoever eats the most of them in 10 minutes. But to rush is an anomaly in the Keys— sit on the large veranda and relax.

KEYS FISHERIES MARKET & MARINA
3502 Gulfview Ave., Marathon: 305-743-4353
keysfisheries.com
CUISINE: Seafood
DRINKS: Full bar
SERVING: Daily lunch and dinner
PRICE RANGE: $$
Not only a marina, but a fish market and a restaurant, too. Similar to those places you see up on Cape Cod where you know the fish is fresh because you can see it in the display case. Lobster Reuben, blackened mahi mahi, fried conch and get a blooming onion. (If you catch your own fish, they'll cook it up for you.)

LAZY DAYS
79867 Overseas Hwy. at MM 79.9, Islamorada: 305-664-5256
http://www.lazydaysrestaurant.com
CUISINE: Seafood/ Bar fare
DRINKS: Full Bar
SERVING: Lunch/ Dinner
PRICE RANGE: $$
As the name implies, this oceanfront eatery is very laid back. Here you'll find outstanding fresh seafood and if you like, the chef will even cook up your own catch. Great happy hour from 4-6 pm.

LORELEI RESTAURANT AND CABANA BAR
81924 Overseas Hwy, Islamorada: 305-664-2692
http://www.loreleicabanabar.com/
CUISINE: Seafood/ Bar fare
DRINKS: Full Bar
SERVING: Breakfast/ Lunch/ Dinner

PRICE RANGE: $$
Big old fish house and bar with great views of the gulf, this is a great place for simple seafood. Great dishes are served up with live music in the evenings.

MARKER 88
88000 Overseas Hwy. at MM 88, Islamorada: 305-852-9315
http://www.marker88.info
CUISINE: Seafood
DRINKS: Full Bar

SERVING: Dinner
PRICE RANGE: $$$
Everything served up here is grown and caught locally. Service might be a little slow but the views and the food are worth it. This is one of those places that makes a great stop when you're driving down to Key West. It's also one of those places where you'll want to propose to whoever you're with, but be careful when gazing into that gorgeous sunset. As nice as Marker 88 is, you can still dress in jeans and flip-flops and not feel out of place.

PIERRE'S
81600 Overseas Hwy. at MM 81.6, Islamorada: 305-664-3225
www.moradabay.com/pierres
CUISINE: French
DRINKS: Full Bar
SERVING: Dinner
PRICE RANGE: $$$$
The décor of this restaurant does not match its cuisine, but that's not a bad thing. Moroccan, African and Indian objets d'art. French food will definitely impress. Dim lights and candlelight offer a unique experience. Want romance? Try the second floor veranda overlooking tiki torches and the ocean.

SNAPPER'S

139 Seaside Ave. at MM 94.5, Key Largo: 305-852-5956

http://www.snapperskeylargo.com

CUISINE: Seafood

DRINKS: Full Bar

SERVING: Lunch/ Dinner

PRICE RANGE: $

A local favorite, this place offers nightly live music for a very casual crowd. Kids love feeding the tarpon off the dock and if you wish, you may fish right there and they will cook up your catch. Free WiFi.

ZIGGIE AND MAD DOG'S

83000 Overseas Hwy., Islamorada: 305-664-3391

http://www.ziggieandmaddogs.com

CUISINE: Steakhouse

DRINKS: Full Bar
SERVING: Dinner
PRICE RANGE: $$$
This casually elegant eatery is friendly and fun.
Owned by former Miami Dolphins player Jim
Mandich, don't be surprised if you run into
Mandich's famous athlete friends.

LOWER KEYS

COCO'S KITCHEN
283 Key Deer Blvd., Big Pine Key: 305-872-4495
http://www.cocoskitchen.com
CUISINE: Cuban/ International
DRINKS: No alcohol
SERVING: Breakfast/ Lunch/ Dinner
PRICE RANGE: $
Don't let the shopping plaza location fool you, this
place serves up everything from black beans and rice
to several pasta dishes. Good food at great prices.

MANGROVE MAMA'S RESTAURANT
19991 Overseas Hwy, Sugarloaf Key: 305-745-3030
http://www.mangrovemamasrestaurant.com
CUISINE: Seafood/ Caribbean
DRINKS: Full Bar
SERVING: Brunch/ Lunch/ Dinner
PRICE RANGE: $$
This place has a true Keys ambiance. Simple tables
shaded by banana trees and palm fronds. They serve

the beer in jelly glasses. Although fish is what's mostly on the menu, you can also have soups, salads and sandwiches. Check out the miniature horses out back.

NO NAME PUB
30813 N Watson Blvd, 1/4 mile south of No Name Bridge, Big Pine Key: 305-872-9115
http://www.nonamepub.com
CUISINE: Pub fare/ Pizza
DRINKS: Full Bar
SERVING: Lunch/ Dinner
PRICE RANGE: $
Funky, old bar in the middle of nowhere. Serves great pizza and subs. Check out their '80s tunes in the old jukebox.

KEY WEST

ALONZO & BERLIN'S LOBSTER HOUSE
A&B LOBSTER HOUSE
700 Front St., Key West: 305-294-5880
http://aandblobsterhouse.com
CUISINE: Seafood
DRINKS: Full Bar
SERVING: Dinner

PRICE RANGE: $$$$
Overall a good restaurant with good food. Seating on the outside offers a beautiful view of the marina. Service is good but can sometimes be a bit rushed.

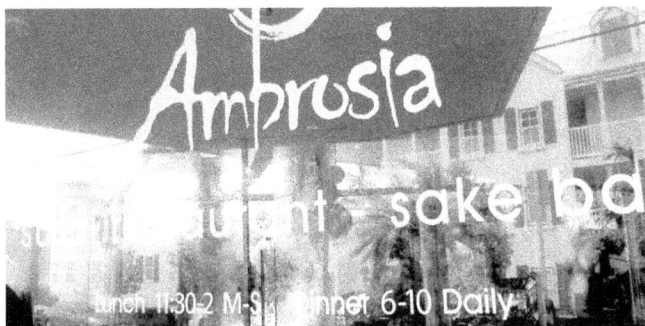

AMBROSIA
1401 Simonton St., Key West: 305-293-0304
http://ambrosiasushi.com/
CUISINE: Sushi
DRINKS: Beer/ Wine
SERVING: Lunch/ Dinner
PRICE RANGE: $
Undoubtedly the best sushi restaurant on the island, this eatery is tucked away in a resort near the beach.

ANTONIA'S
615 Duval St., Key West: 305-294-6565
http://www.antoniaskeywest.com
CUISINE: Italian
DRINKS: Full Bar
SERVING: Dinner
PRICE RANGE: $$$
Great place for the traditional Italian favorites. Pastas are homemade and the ambience is quaint and cozy.

AZUR

425 Grinnell St., Key West: 305-292-2987
www.azurkeywest.com
CUISINE: American (New), Mediterranean
DRINKS: Beer & Wine
SERVING: Breakfast, Lunch & Dinner.
PRICE RANGE: $$
Dine in a beautiful blue dining room or on a shaded terrace. This restaurant serves a delicious selection of Mediterranean specialties. Great seafood, atmosphere, and service.

BAD BOY BURRITO

1128 Simonton St., Key West: 305-292-2697
http://www.badboyburrito.com
CUISINE: Mexican
DRINKS: No alcohol
SERVING: Lunch/ Dinner
PRICE RANGE: $
Great burritos and great tacos, not many places to sit so take-out is probably best. Closes 10pm.

BAGATELLE

115 Duval St., Key West: 305-296-6609
http://www.bagatellekeywest.com
CUISINE: Seafood, Tropical
DRINKS: Full Bar
SERVING: Lunch/ Dinner
PRICE RANGE: $$$
Take a seat on the second-floor veranda and you will have a great view for people watching on ever-busy

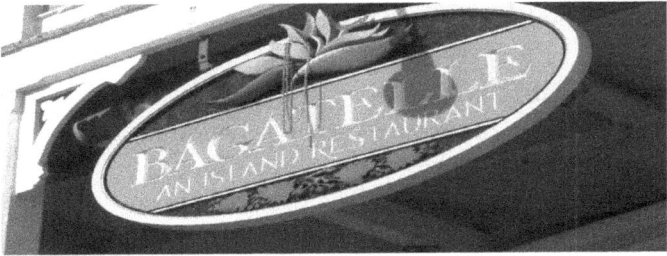

Duval Street. All the dishes here, including chicken and beef, are given the tropical treatment.

BANANA CAFÉ
1215 Duval St., Key West: 305-294-7227
www.bananacafekw.com
CUISINE: French
DRINKS: Beer/ Wine
SERVING: Breakfast/ Lunch/ Dinner
PRICE RANGE: $$
This Country French local café has a strong, loyal clientele. Great food at affordable prices. Live jazz on Thursday nights.

BLUE HEAVEN
729 Thomas St., Key West: 305-296-8666
http://www.blueheavenkw.com
CUISINE: Seafood, American
DRINKS: Full Bar
SERVING: Breakfast/ Lunch/ Dinner
PRICE RANGE: $$
You can't get more "Key West" than this hippie-run restaurant that has some of the best food in town. Be prepared to wait in line. Don't let the dirty floors and roaming cats and birds put you off; give this place a

shot. They say Hemingway (a big boxing fan) used to referee matches here every Friday night.

B.O.'S FISH WAGON
801 Caroline St., Key West: 305-294-9272
bosfishwagon.com
CUISINE: Seafood
DRINKS: Beer / Wine
SERVING: Daily lunch and dinner
PRICE RANGE: $$
You can't get more Keys lifestyle than this—there's nothing more to this dump than a tawdry little shack where the walls are covered with old rusty license plates, fishnets, sponges, buoys that have seen better days. (Some of the customers have seen better days, too.) There's even a rusted out old truck outside. But who cares? People have a great time here. The menu is limited, mainly to fried fish sandwiches (grouper, daily catch, soft shell crab, shrimp or cracked conch) and a very good chili dog, but the standout here would be the conch fritters. Somebody's always pounding away on the piano and after a while people get up and start dancing.

THE CAFÉ, A MOSTLY VEGETARIAN PLACE
509 Southard St., Key West: 305-296-5515
www.thecafekw.com
CUISINE: Vegetarian
DRINKS: Beer/ Wine
SERVING: Lunch/ Dinner
PRICE RANGE: $
Not a vegetarian? Neither am I, but this place proves you don't have to be in order to enjoy the great food.

Favorites include homemade soups and veggie burgers. Their Sunday brunch is worth checking out.

CAFÉ MARQUESA
600 Fleming St., Key West: 305-292-1919
http://www.marquesa.com
CUISINE: Contemporary American
DRINKS: Full Bar
SERVING: Dinner
PRICE RANGE: $$$$
Intimate, cozy restaurant with amazing food and fantastic service. They close for two weeks during summer so call ahead. Reservations are suggested.

CAFÉ SOLÉ
1029 Southard St., Key West: 305-294-0230
http://www.cafesole.com
CUISINE: French
DRINKS: Wine/ Beer
SERVING: Dinner
PRICE RANGE: $$$
Great place to find a taste of France, tucked away in a residential neighborhood. Mutton snapper in wine is great and the bouillabaisse is pretty damned good. Latticework against the walls gives this place the kind of Key West ambiance you come down here to experience. Cozy, intimate, charming.

COMMODORE WATERFRONT
700 Front St., Key West: 305-294-9191
www.commodorekeywest.com
CUISINE: Steakhouse
DRINKS: Full Bar
SERVING: Dinner
PRICE RANGE: $$$

Two levels of dining, downstairs is the Boathouse and upstairs is the Commodore, offering excellent selection of steaks and seafood. Warm atmosphere, great service.

CONCH REPUBLIC SEAFOOD CO.
631 Greene St., Key West: 305-294-4403
www.conchrepublicseafood.com
CUISINE: Seafood
DRINKS: Full Bar
SERVING: Lunch, Dinner
PRICE RANGE: $$
An open-air restaurant overlooking the historic seaport and the Key West Marina. Waterfront dining with a menu that features Caribbean influenced cuisine and of course great seafood. Live music, good service.

CROISSANTS DE FRANCE
816 Duval St., Key West: 305-294-2624
www.croissantsdefrance.com
CUISINE: Bakery, French Café
DRINKS: Beer & Wine
SERVING: Breakfast, Lunch, Dinner
PRICE RANGE: $$
Bistro on one side, bakery on the other. Great fresh baked croissants, delicious crepes, pastries, soups and sandwiches. Patio dining.

CUBAN COFFEE QUEEN
284 Margaret St, Key West, 305-292-4747
www.cubancoffeequeen.com
CUISINE: Cuban/Breakfast

DRINKS: No Booze
SERVING: Breakfast, Lunch & Dinner
PRICE RANGE: $
Popular Cuban counter-serve spot that offers great
Cuban coffee drinks and traditional Cuban fare. Daily
specials.

DJ'S CLAM SHACK

629 Duval St., Key West: 305-294-0102
http://www.djsclamshack.com
CUISINE: American/ Seafood
DRINKS: Beer/ Wine
SERVING: Lunch/ Dinner
PRICE RANGE: $
Not fancy, just awesome! Informal eating at its best,
you will be blown away by their lobster roll, clams
and conch fritters. Friendly service and budget
friendly.

DUFFY'S STEAK & LOBSTER HOUSE

1007 Simonton St., Key West: 305-296-4900
www.duffyskeywest.com
CUISINE: Steakhouse, Seafood
DRINKS: Full Bar

SERVING: Dinner
PRICE RANGE: $$$
Italian steak and lobster house offering a menu that includes a variety of seafood including dolphin. A locals' favorite. Good food, good service.

FIRST FLIGHT ISLAND RESTAURANT & BREWERY
301 Whitehead St, Key West, 305-293-8484
www.firstflightkw.com
CUISINE: American (New)

DRINKS: Full Bar
SERVING: Lunch, dinner; one of the best happy hours in town
PRICE RANGE: $$
Located in the former location of Kelly's Caribbean Bar, this newly decorated venue offers a casual eatery serving American fare. Creative cocktails. Brewery with 3 of their own brews on tap. Live music some nights.

FIVE BROTHERS GROCERY AND SANDWICH SHOP
930 Southard St (at Grinnell), Key West, 305-296-5205
NO WEBSITE
CUISINE: Grocery / Cuban
DRINKS: No Booze
SERVING: Daily 6-6; closed Sun
PRICE RANGE: $
Next to a very downmarket laundromat is the popular grocery and sandwich shop combination that is a favorite of locals and tourists. Run by a Cuban, so the food is good food and so is the café con leche. Munch on guava pastries and ham croquettes. There's a really lip-smacking breakfast sandwich with ham, eggs and cheese on Cuban bread pressed thin. BBQ Pork Sandwich and the Fried Grouper sandwich.

FRENCHIE'S CAFÉ
529 United St., Key West: 305-900-396-7124
www.frenchieskeywest.com
CUISINE: French, Café
DRINKS: No Alcohol

SERVING: Breakfast, Lunch
PRICE RANGE: $
Great inexpensive place for breakfast or lunch.
Delicious, fresh sandwiches. Great coffee. Friendly
service.

GLAZED DONUTS
420 Eaton St, Key West, 305-294-9142
www.glazeddonuts.com
CUISINE: Donuts / Cafe
DRINKS: No Booze
SERVING: Breakfast & Lunch
PRICE RANGE: $$
Not your typical donut shop, these are the ultimate
deluxe donuts – key lime custard cream and chocolate
covered are the best. All donuts made from scratch.

HALF SHELL RAW BAR
231 Margaret St, Key West, 305-294-7496
www.halfshellrawbar.com
CUISINE: Seafood
DRINKS: Full Bar
SERVING: Lunch & Dinner
PRICE RANGE: $$
Set in a former shrimp-packing facility, this casual
fish shack features waterside seating on picnic tables.
The décor is pretty minimalistic—lots of license
plates from all over the world are nailed to the walls.
At twilight you'll be able to watch as boats leave the
marina for their "sunset cruises." Happy hour brings
ridiculous low prices for beers and oysters on the half
shell. Menu includes: Gulf oysters, stuffed shrimp,

and stuffed snapper. Hang out and enjoy the shuffleboard tables.

HOT TIN ROOF
Ocean Key Resort & Spa
0 Duval St., Key West: 305-296-7701
http://www.oceankey.com/key-west-restaurant
CUISINE: International Fusion
DRINKS: Full Bar
SERVING: Dinner
PRICE RANGE: $$$$
Offering indoor and outdoor deck seating overlooking the harbor, this restaurant is the epitome of casual elegance. Here, the menu is a bit of a mixed bag, with French, Asian and South American specialties. Reserve ahead in season.

ISLAND DOGS BAR
505 Front St., Key West: 305-509-7136
http://www.islanddogsbar.com
CUISINE: American
DRINKS: Full Bar
SERVING: Lunch/ Dinner
PRICE RANGE: $
Not what you would typically expect from bar food, this place has delicious burgers, chicken fingers and chicken wings. Great people watching.

LA TE DA
1125 Duval St., Key West: 305-296-6706
lateda.com
CUISINE: American
DRINKS: Full bar

SERVING: Lunch, dinner
PRICE RANGE: $$$
Super place for lunch or dinner. The atmosphere is just great, eating outside under the trees by the pool. Or on the balcony. Omelet cake with pancetta, fontina cheese, arugula, oven roasted tomatoes and spinach, oysters remoulade and scallops wrapped in Serano ham, rosemary and mustard-crusted pork tenderloin, tamarind-glazed lamb loin and garlic shrimp served over polenta. Yum.

LA TRATTORIA
524 Duval St., Key West: 305-296-1075
http://www.latrattoria.us
CUISINE: Italian
DRINKS: Full Bar
SERVING: Dinner
PRICE RANGE: $$$
True traditional Italian dishes served in a relaxed atmosphere. Staff is very friendly. Stop by their cocktail lounge, Virgilio's, for live jazz until 2am.

Lattitudes Beach Cafe

LATITUDES BEACH CAFÉ

245 Front St., Key West: 305-292-5300

www.sunsetkeycottages.com

CUISINE: Caribbean, Seafood, Mexican

DRINKS: Full Bar

SERVING: Breakfast/ Lunch/ Dinner

PRICE RANGE: $$$$

Very nice atmosphere in this scenic restaurant. The food is good and the service is friendly. Try sitting at the bar at sunset for a wow factor.

LOUIE'S BACKYARD

700 Waddell Ave., Key West: 305-294-1061

http://www.louiesbackyard.com

CUISINE: Caribbean

DRINKS: Full Bar

SERVING: Lunch/ Dinner

PRICE RANGE: $$$$

Truly one of the most romantic restaurants around, the fact that it's located off the beaten path just lends to the charm. Dishes are the creation of famed Chef Norman Van Aken, sunset cocktails are ideal at the oceanfront tiki bar. Reserve ahead.

MANGIA, MANGIA

900 Southard St., Key West: 305-294-2469

http://www.mangia-mangia.com

CUISINE: Italian

DRINKS: Beer/ Wine

SERVING: Dinner

PRICE RANGE: $$

Off the beaten path, this place serves up homemade pastas and tasty marinara sauce. Relax out back in their charming patio with a glass of wine or a beer from their rather large selection.

MANGOES
700 Duval St., Key West: 305-294-8002
www.mangoeskeywest.com/
CUISINE: American, Seafood
DRINKS: Beer/ Wine
SERVING: Lunch/ Dinner/ Late night
PRICE RANGE: $$$
The brick patio shaded by the canopy of large banyan trees makes this place packed almost every day. Even though it's located on touristy Duval Street, check out the back bar for a locals loungy scene.

MARTIN'S
917 Duval St., Key West: 305-295-0111
http://www.martinskeywest.com
CUISINE: American/German
DRINKS: Full Bar
SERVING: Dinner/ Sunday brunch
PRICE RANGE: $$$$
Very elegant dining in a contemporary setting. Indoor/outdoor. Has some German specialties like Duck Breast "Schwarzwald" (grilled duck breast served in a Burgundy sauce, with red cabbage and rosemary potatoes, garnished with a poached pear half & Lingonberry marmalade and Jäger Schnitzel (Wiener Schnitzel topped with a mushroom sauce and served with Spätzle. But I end up going for the lamb osso bucco. Also excellent seafood and pasta dishes. And here you can get Maine lobster, a welcome relief

from the ubiquitous Florida variety. Apple strudel for dessert is a must.

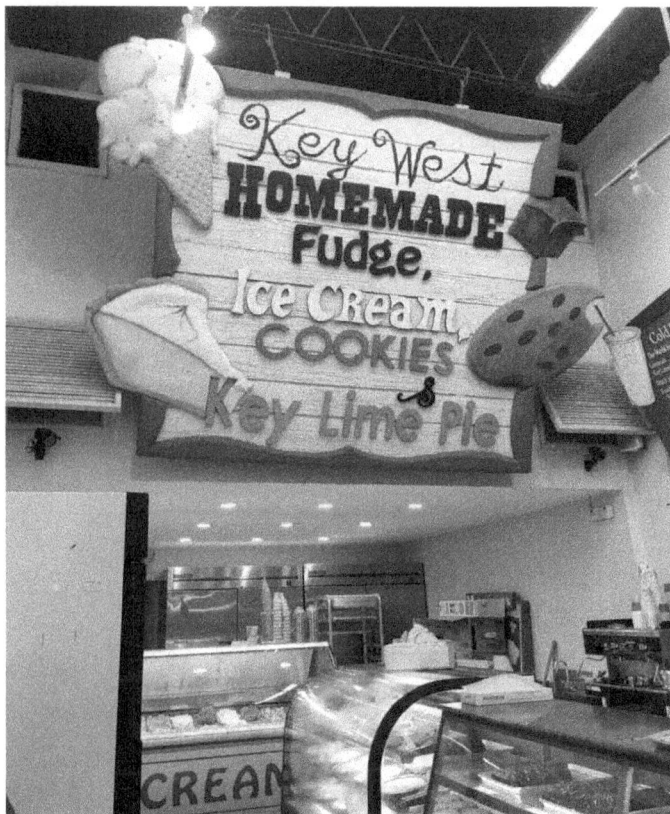

MATTHEESSEN'S 4TH OF JULY ICE CREAM PARLOR
419 Duval St & 106 Duval St, Key West, 305-923-5418
http://mattskeywest.com/
CUISINE: American/ Desserts
DRINKS: No alcohol

SERVING: Lunch/ Dinner
PRICE RANGE: $
For junk food junkies. Serving up humongous portions of ice cream (one is enough to share) and incredible monster cookies, this place also offers great hamburgers and fries, grilled cheese sandwiches, onion rings and club wraps.

MR Z'S
501 Southard St., Key Wes: 305-296-4445
http://www.mrzskeywest.com
CUISINE: American
DRINKS: Beer/ Wine
SERVING: Lunch/ Dinner/ Late night
PRICE RANGE: $
Great pizza, great cheesesteak sandwich but terrible service and even worse is their delivery.

NINE ONE FIVE BISTRO & WINE BAR
915 Duval St., Key West: 305-296-0669
www.915duval.com
CUISINE: American, Seafood
DRINKS: Full Bar
SERVING: Dinner
PRICE RANGE: $$$
Great place for watching the sunset on the porch. Excellent service and great food choices like the filet mignon beef carpaccio and stone crab.

ONLYWOOD PIZZERIA TRATTORIA
613 ½ Duval St. (in rear), Key West: 305-735-4412
www.onlywoodkw.com
CUISINE: Italian

DRINKS: Beer / Wine
SERVING: Daily lunch and dinner
PRICE RANGE: $$
Tucked between (and behind) 2 buildings off frenetic
Duval Street is this completely delightful "find"
where you can smell oregano and basil growing in the
garden. The pizza here is cooked in a wood-burning
oven sent over from Naples. Locals come here for
the excellent pizza. They make their own mozzarella,
which is understandably featured on many of their
pies along with items such an anchovies, sausage, etc.
Seafood pizzas are very good: Key West shrimp,
clams, calamari, scallops.

PANINI PANINI
1075 Duval St., Key West: 305-296-2002
http://www.paninikw.com
CUISINE: Sandwiches/ Vegetarian/ Smoothies
DRINKS: Beer/ Wine
SERVING: Breakfast/ Lunch/ Dinner
PRICE RANGE: $
The food is really good and very reasonably priced.
Fresh baked bread and a great selection of drinks and
smoothies. Friendly staff.

PEPE'S
806 Caroline St., Key West: 305-294-7192
http://pepescafe.net
CUISINE: American
DRINKS: Full Bar
SERVING: Breakfast/ Lunch/ Dinner
PRICE RANGE: $$

Good, basic food includes steak, oysters, chili, fish sandwiches and burgers. You will enjoy this rustic eatery with historical Key West photos on the walls.

SANDY'S CAFÉ
1026 White St., Key West: 305-296-4747
http://sandyscafe.com/
CUISINE: Cuban; Seafood; Deli
DRINKS: No booze
SERVING: Open 24 hours
PRICE RANGE: $
When you see the sign reading M&M Laundry, you know you're there. It's just a little take-out window, but if you hanker for an honest-to-God Cuban sandwich (ham, pork, lettuce and pickles—get extra mustard), this is the place in Key West to get it. You'll commonly see police and fire rescue personnel here at all hours. Why? It's good. And it's cheap.

SANTIAGO'S BODEGA
207 Petronia St., Suite 101, Key West: 305-296-7691
http://www.santiagosbodega.com
CUISINE: Tapas/ Small Plates
DRINKS: Beer/ Wine
SERVING: Lunch/ Dinner
PRICE RANGE: $$$
Off the beaten path and away from the crowds, this great eatery is located in the Bahama Village. Excellent selection of small dishes and both hot and cold tapas like smoked salmon carpaccio with crostini, crème fraiche, capers, and minced onions, tomato and basil bruschetta with olive tapenade on crostini, yellowfin ceviche, marinated in spicy citrus

juice and served with avocado, mango, and cilantro, the trio (traditional hummus, roasted red pepper hummus, and black olive tapenade) served with pita bread, Roman meatballs in a nest of angel hair pasta, pinchos morunos, spicy marinated skewers of pork tenderloin with apple-mango chutney, beef tenderloin, seared and topped with bleu cheese butter, croquettas, cayenne spiced pan-fried patties of potatoes, house ground prosciutto and provolone cheese with scallion cream, lamb patties, ground leg of lamb, fresh thyme, sherry, and lemon zest with a cucumber and feta salad. Their sangria is a must have.

SARABETH'S
530 Simonton St., Key West: 305-293-8181
http://sarabethskeywest.com
CUISINE: American
DRINKS: Full Bar
SERVING: Breakfast/ Lunch/ Dinner
PRICE RANGE: $$

An offshoot of the famed New York City hotspot, here you will find delicious breakfasts with their homemade jams and jellies. For lunch and dinner, you will find everything from Caesar salad to burgers to chicken pot pie.

SEVEN FISH
Truman Ave., Key West: 305-296-2777
http://www.7fish.com
CUISINE: Seafood
DRINKS: Full Bar
SERVING: Dinner
PRICE RANGE: $$$
Favorite seafood restaurant amongst locals: "simple, good food" is their motto.

SOUTHERNMOST BEACH CAFE
1405 Duval St., Key West: 305-295-6550
http://www.southernmostbeachcafe.com
CUISINE: American
DRINKS: Full Bar
SERVING: Breakfast/ Lunch/ Dinner
PRICE RANGE: $
Incredible views, incredible food and incredible prices. This place has a great cheap breakfast. Service might be a little slow. Great happy hour specials.

TAVERN N TOWN
3841 N. Roosevelt Blvd., Key West: 305-296-8100
www.tavernntown.com
CUISINE: Floribbean/ International
DRINKS: Full Bar
SERVING: Lunch/ Dinner

PRICE RANGE: $$$$
Another creation of famed chef Norman Van Aken, here you will find everything from seafood and steak to vegetable pad Thai. There is also a selection of tapas and small plates.

THAI CUISINE
513 Greene St., Key West: 305-294-9424
www.keywestthaicuisine.com WEBSITE DOWN AT PRESSTIME
CUISINE: Thai
DRINKS: Full Bar
SERVING: Lunch & Dinner
PRICE RANGE: $$
Thai cuisine and sushi with variety of vegetarian options. Service not great but the good is good. Off the beaten path location.

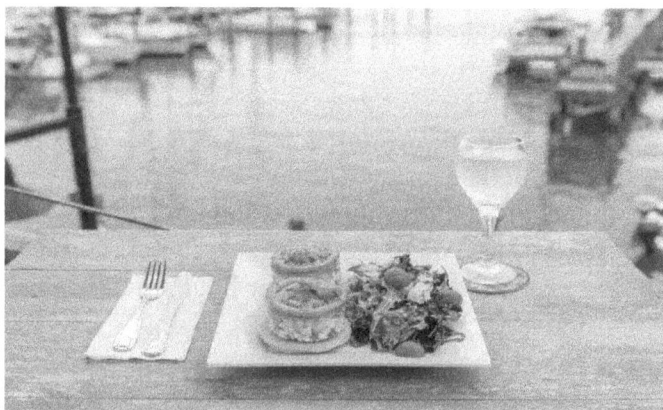

TURTLE KRAALS RESTAURANT & BAR
231 Margaret St., Key West: 305-294-2640
http://www.turtlekraals.com

CUISINE: Southwestern/ Seafood
DRINKS: Full Bar
SERVING: Lunch/ Dinner
PRICE RANGE: $$
This converted warehouse with indoor and dockside seating has something for everyone. Kids will especially like the wildlife exhibits that include a turtle cannery.

WHITE STREET SANDWICH SHOP
1222 White St, Key West, 305-797-6871
www.thebestcoffeeintown.net
CUISINE: Cuban / Deli
DRINKS: No Booze
SERVING: 5 a.m. – 6 p.m. daily
PRICE RANGE: $
Right in the heart of the Key West seaport, this street shop sells great Cuban sandwiches, superior Cuban coffee and an excellent mound of pulled pork with rice & beans.

Chapter 4
NIGHTLIFE

UPPER & MIDDLE KEYS

Nightlife in the Keys pretty much translates into the
word: "bar." There just ain't nothin' else to do.
There's no theatre, no culture of any kind (except for
some hit or miss things in Key West).

HOG HEAVEN

85361 Overseas Hwy. at MM 85.3, Islamorada: 305-664-9669

http://www.hogheavensportsbar.com

This waterside biker bar has big screen TVs, video games and pool tables. Most patrons are regulars. Open daily from 11am to 4am.

TIKI BAR AT THE HOLIDAY ISLE RESORT

84001 Overseas Hwy. at MM 84, Islamorada: 305-664-2321

http://www.holidayisle.com
This place offers booze, dancing and a great time practically at any time of the day. Equal mix of tourists and locals.

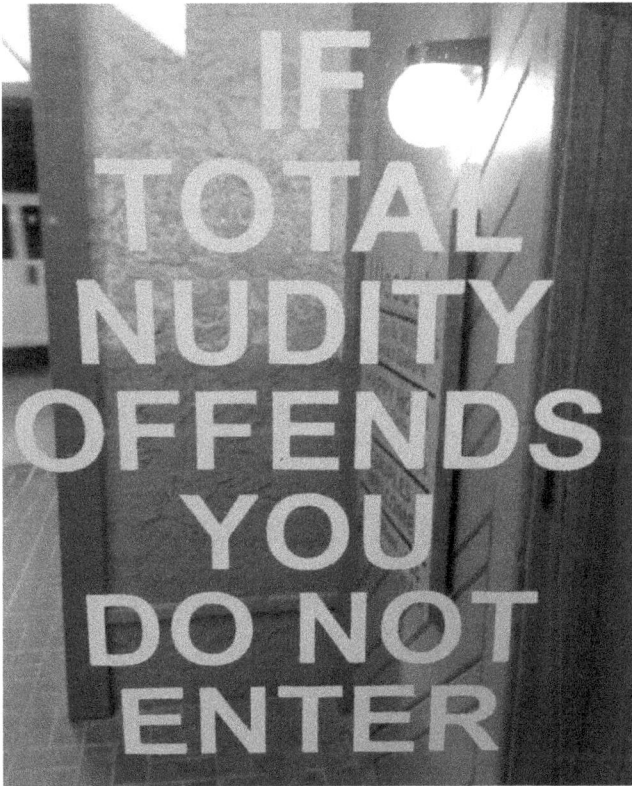

WOODY'S IN THE KEYS
81908 Overseas Hwy. at MM 82, Islamorada: 305-664-0059
http://www.woodysinthekeys.com

Wacky, loud and raunchy; this place is not for the faint of heart. With buck-naked strippers and a live band, this place also has a show that highlights a 300-pound native American who does a rude and crude routine of politically incorrect jokes. You've been warned.

NIGHTLIFE
Key West

AQUA
711 Duval St., Key West: 305-294-0555
http://www.aquakeywest.com
Very friendly gay bar, this place welcomes everybody. Don't be shy and step inside, you will love their drag shows. Great dance floor and great music in a very sociable environment.

BLUE MOJITO POOL BAR & GRILL

Hyatt Key West Resort and Spa
601 Front St., Key West, 305-809-1234
https://keywest.centric.hyatt.com
Enjoy cocktails overlooking the Gulf of Mexico in
this sophisticated Key West bar. Great daily happy
hour specials. Live music.

BOTTLECAP LOUNGE & LIQUOR STORE

1128 Simonton St., Key West: 305-296-2807
http://www.bottlecapkeywest.com
Great dive bar. This place has it all: Top DJs, live
music, dance bar, music videos, lounge area, patio bar
and pool tables. Some of the seating in the lounge
area can be quite intimate, or at least as intimate as
you can get in this kind of rowdy establishment.

BOURBON STREET PUB

724 Duval St., Key West: 305-294-9354
http://www.bourbonstreetpub.com

Techno and alternative music pumps out to a gay/straight mixed crowd. Great place to dance and people watch. There is also a pool and garden bar if you need a break from the dance floor.

CAPTAIN TONY'S SALOON
428 Greene St., Key West: 305-294-1838
http://www.capttonyssaloon.com
Once a morgue, this spirited bar is said to have been home to the original Sloppy Joe's, having entertained author Ernest Hemingway. Rustic and smoky, check out the "hanging tree" located inside the bar.

CORK & STOGIE CIGAR AND WINE BAR
1218 Duval St., Key West: 305-517-6419
www.corkandstogie.com

Friendly place to drink and smoke cigars if that's your thing. Small front porch for relaxing. Great wine selection.

COWBOY BILL'S HONKY TONK SALOON
618 Duval St., Key West: 305-292-1865
http://www.cowboybillskw.net/
A country-western sports bar with a mechanical bull. A rowdy crowd and lots of games including pool, darts, & video games. 27 TVs for watching sports. Live music.

D'VINE WINE GALLERY @ THE GARDENS HOTEL
526 Angela St., Key West: 305-294-2661
www.gardenshotel.com
A unique state-of-the-art wine tasting bar that offers up 32 bottles for sampling. Cabaret nights on Thursdays & Live Jazz in the Gardens on Sundays.

GARDEN OF EDEN
224 Duval St., Key West: 305-296-4565
www.bullkeywest.com/GARDENcoupon.asp
Two flights up on the side of the building, this bar is completely clothing optional. During the day, you will find sun worshippers vying for the perfect tan and at night, you will find a great mix of people (some of them opting for the no clothing alternative) enjoying the bird's eye view of the debauchery on Duval Street.

GRAND VIN WINE SHOP & BAR
1107 Duval St., Key West: 305-296-1020
A casual inviting wine shop and bar with a nice selection of wines. Hang out with the regulars or relax on the porch overlooking Duval Street.

GREEN PARROT BAR
601 Whitehead St., Key West: 305-294-6133
http://www.greenparrot.com
Green Parrot is more than a bar; it's a Key West icon. Known as an open-air hipster watering hole, there's

live music on most nights. Locals' hangout. Legend has it Hemingway used to stop here on his walk home after leaving Sloppy Joe's. (And it looks like they haven't changed anything since.)

HOG'S BREATH SALOON
400 Front St., Key West: 305-296-4222
http://www.hogsbreath.com
This place is right across the street form Mallory Square, ground zero for sunset festivities. Live entertainment goes on daily, as well as the raucous partying. Friendly staff.

LA TE DA
La Te Da Hotel, 1125 Duval St., Key West: 305-296-6706
http://www.lateda.com
Located in the La Te Da Hotel, with three great bars, the outside Terrace Bar, the inside Piano Bar, and the upstairs Crystal Bar. Has a popular drag revue. Tourists and locals frequent these gay establishments (you don't have to be gay to enjoy the shows). The

sheer gorgeousness of this place overshadows the excellent food they turn out.

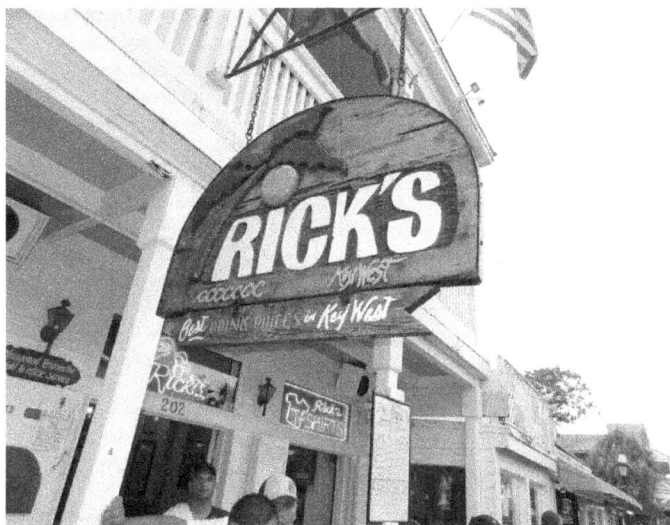

RICK'S BAR
202 Duval St., Key West: 305-296-5513
www.ricksanddurtyharrys.com
Complex with **eight** unique bars. Live music (and a hell of a lot more) every night. Late night karaoke every night at midnight. Drink specials.
THE ORIGINAL RICK'S BAR
This is the place that got the whole complex started.
RED GARTER SALOON
Adult entertainment. Strippers, etc., 2 big bars, 2 stages with nude dancing, 6 "champagne rooms" upstairs and a handful of "private dance booths." (I think you get the idea).
DURTY HARRY'S
Rock music venue live performances every night.

RICK'S UPSTAIRS

This is the dance club with DJs knocking out disco music, with a light show and all the bells and whistles.

MARDI GRAS DAIQUIRI BAR

Serves 8 flavors of those frozen daiquiris that make college kids throw up all over the place. A charming experience, especially during Spring Break.

TREE BAR

If you want to people-watch on the street, choose this place. Quality cocktails mixed by real bartenders who can do more than pump out frozen Slurpee-type flavored drinks with grain alcohol. Big shade tree helps attract a breeze in warm weather.

LOFT

Go through Rick's Upstairs and slide into the Loft, which is where you'll get quality martinis. And wines by the glass. This is the bar I actually like the best out of all of them here at Rick's. A little class among the dreck.

CROW'S NEST

Above the madness where the music is playing below at Durty Harry's is this sequestered deck that lets you look down on everybody. Of course, there's a bar wherever you turn. These people are making a killing. God bless them.

RUM BAR AT THE SPEAKEASY INN

1117 Duval St., Key West: 305-296-2680
www.speakeasyinn.com
Small hotel bar with a comfortable atmosphere. Very friendly. Great place to start the night.

SCHOONER WHARF BAR
202 William, Key West: 305-292-3302
www.schoonerwharf.com
A locals' favorite located on the water. Boat-like ambiance. Great seafood. Live music. Two happy hours.

SMOKIN' TUNA SALOON
4 Charles St., Key West: 305-517-6350
www.smokintunasaloon.com
Very friendly bar (crowd and bartender) with live music, fresh seafood & raw bar. Outdoor seating.

INDEX

69

DID YOU FIND AN INTERESTING PLACE?

If you discover a place you think I should check out on my next visit, drop me a line, will you? I'll mention your name if I end up listing it.

andrewdelaplaine@mac.com

WANT 3 **FREE** THRILLERS?

Why, of course you do!

If you like these writers--
Vince Flynn, Brad Thor, Tom Clancy, James Patterson, David Baldacci, John Grisham, Brad Meltzer, Daniel Silva, Don DeLillo

If you like these TV series --
House of Cards, Scandal, West Wing, The Good Wife, Madam Secretary, Designated Survivor

You'll love the **unputdownable** series about
Jack Houston St. Clair, with political intrigue, romance,
suspense.

Besides writing travel books, I've written political thrillers
for many years that have delighted hundreds of thousands
of readers. I want to introduce you to my work!
Send me an email and I'll send you a link where you can
download the first 3 books in my bestselling series,
absolutely FREE.

Mention **this book** when you email me.

andrewdelaplaine@mac.com